Flower Power

BOUQUETS AND SIMPLE ARRANGEMENTS

Flower Power

BOUQUETS AND SIMPLE ARRANGEMENTS

by Malin Hidesäter

Photographs by Anna Skoog

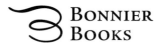

BONNIER
BOOKS

Bonnier Books, Appledram Barns, Birdham Road,
Chichester, PO20 7EQ, UK

www.bonnierbooks.co.uk

First published in the UK in 2008 by Bonnier Books
ISBN: 978-1-905825-78-3

© 2007 Albert Bonniers Förlag AB, Stockholm
© 2007 Malin Hidesäter, text, and Anna Skoog, photographs

First published by Albert Bonniers Förlag AB, Stockholm, Sweden

Published in the English language by arrangement with
Bonnier Group Agency, Stockholm, Sweden

Translated by Åsa Hjelmberg

Printed in China

Contents

Introduction: more flowers to the people!

The idea for Flower Power *came about because we both love cut flowers and want to share our simple creations. The book could have been many pages longer because there are hundreds of gorgeous flowers to play with but we've selected our absolute favourites, nothing fancy; they all use flowers that you can easily find in most flower shops.*

We have revelled in creating beautiful flower arrangements and bouquets that are quite irresistible. From our own experience we know that you can make a simple bouquet or table decoration while the dinner is cooking and the children – and the neighbours' children, and probably some energetic dogs too – are demanding your attention.

There are endless ways of decorating with flowers. With this book we hope to awaken the desire in you to create bouquets and gifts for loved ones and to provide fresh ideas and inspirations for combinations and arrangements. All you need is the passion and the will to experiment freely and you'll soon be a flower expert yourself.

Malin and Anna

Good advice

Buying cut flowers in a flower shop is simple. You benefit from the professional help of the florist who will advise on your choice, tie your bouquet or make a beautiful arrangement. But, once home, how do you care for the flowers to ensure that they stay fresh for longer?

These are my ground rules:
- Always re-cut the flower stems if they have been out of water for a while and use a sharp knife. If, however, your florist has put wet paper around the stems or stuck them in wet foam, you won't need to re-cut.
- Remove all leaves that would otherwise end up below the water level.
- Use a clean vase.
- Change the water frequently. You often find a little bag of plant nourishment provided with your flowers. Use it, then change water after a day or two – there will be no need for more nourishment.

By following these simple guidelines you give cut flowers their best chance but still you can never know exactly for how long they will last. I've often heard people comment that although their florist assured them their roses would last for a week they faded after four days. What could be the reason? Well, flowers are alive after all and, just like people, they react differently to their environment. Certainly if you place flowers in a very warm room, for example, they will not last long.

As you read through this book you'll pick up a few tricks to use for certain flowers that will make them give of their best.

Good luck!

Tools and equipment

- Knife (preferably a florist's knife)
- Pruning shears
- Scissors
- Different kinds of wire and raffia for tying your bouquets

All these tools are available from flower shops or garden centres.

Oasis

Florist's foam, often sold as Oasis, is used when you require stability in an arrangement. It is easy to work with and comes in different colours and shapes.

Cut the foam into the shape you desire. (Do not resist the temptation to press down your fingers in the leftovers!) Put the foam in water to soak, but don't force it under the water, because that will create air bubbles. After about an hour it will be ready for use.

Spiral hand-tied bouquet

When I went to florist school in Tvååker in southwest Sweden we were taught how to make a hand-tied bouquet. Oh, this was difficult the first few times, with fingers and stems pointing in all directions! Luckily for me I have big hands (thank you for that grandmother). Once you've mastered this method it is much easier to make a beautiful bouquet.
Here's how to do it.

Place two flowers together so they cross over two-thirds of the way down the stem.

Add in one flower at a time, placing each new flower to the right of the one on top. After you've added in several new flowers you'll notice you have created a spiral shape.

Tie the bouquet with raffia right where you kept your thumb. Above this point you will have the bouquet and beneath, the stems will splay out attractively in the vase.

11

Here comes spring!

And long have we waited! The bicycle is dusted off, the clogs come out, and the streets get swept. Best of all, the flower shops are filled with spring flowers, especially brightly coloured tulips. We Swedes are rather good at buying tulips – we actually hold the world record! If you are lucky you can find yourself in a flower shop that has a few unusual ones. Once you start to recognise the different varieties of tulips it can be fun to learn their names. Maybe a Bruno Liljefors is your favourite?

Libretto Parrot, Orange Princess, Valery Gergier, Baby Doll, Ballerina, Red Princess, Bruno Liljefors, Yellow Flight, Webers Parrot, Salmon Parrot and Rembrandt.

Hyacinths, narcissi and the Libretto Parrot tulips.

French tulip, Monte Carlo and Blenda.

Red Princess, Tailleux, Rembrandt, Gerard Dou, Baby Doll and Ballerina.

13

The tulip Orange Princess.

A small party bouquet with anemones, snowball bush and various tulips.

Beloved tulips

Sometimes it is really hard to decide because there are so many different tulips to choose from. But why pick one when you can have several? Double, single, feathered or flamed – just mix and match. Place the flowers in your cream jugs, crystal vases or china cups. Grandmother's coffee set may finally come into use!

Offer a whole arrangement as a gift, complete with vase!
The tulip Webers Parrot with sprigs of cherry blossom just in bloom.

The tulip Ingell, white germini (small gerbera) and broom.

Easter decorations

For me, Easter is the best holiday of the year because of the colours associated with it. I couldn't agree with anyone who doesn't like yellow. No other colour brings out such desire in me to go out and buy flowers. Just think of daffodils! Those long green stalks lying in boxes in the grocery store in spring are like ugly ducklings. They may not look like much until they brilliantly transform into beautiful sun-yellow trumpets. Then there are grape hyacinths, mimosa and irises that also light up our Easter.

Narcissus, grape hyacinth, mimosa and snowdrop.

Narcissus, ranunculus and mimosa.

Mimosa, double narcissus, ranunculus and iris.

Easter in bloom

The contents of an Easter egg can be swiftly transformed with a piece of foam and a few fresh flowers. Line the base of one half of a pretty cardboard egg with a piece of plastic. Fill it with soaked foam. Cut the stems of your flowers to a suitable length and poke them into the foam, taking care to hide it completely with the blooms. Here the egg is filled with ranunculus, grape hyacinths, mimosa and narcissi. PS Eat the sweets first!

23

A tiered cake plate for the Easter table with ranunculus, narcissus, grape hyacinth and mimosa.

The wonderful thing about tulips is that you can see that they are alive. They seem to grow like mad, especially if they are in a lot of water. Personally, I find them more beautiful when they spill gracefully over the edge of the container, like this armful of French tulips, than when they stand up perfectly straight in a vase.

Cut flowers can be transformed into potted plants in a matter of minutes. Buy a pot of the pearlwort Sagina procumbens, which looks like a miniature lawn, put it into a terracotta pot and water it. Make small holes with a stick and poke ranunculus, cut to different lengths, into the holes, taking care not to break the flower heads. Entwine some small pussy willow twigs around the rim of the pot, and secure with wire. Don't forget to water your pot plant!

The flower that became a potted plant.

Soak a ball of florist's foam in water for about an hour. Cut the stems on a bunch of feverfew to within 2–3 cm of the flower heads. One by one, press the flowers closely together into the foam until it is completely covered. Place the ball on a pretty plate and water the plate from time to time.

The flower ball

Soak a foam ring upside down in water for about an hour. Cut the stems on twenty or so carnations to about 4 centimetres. Press the flowers closely together into the foam until it is completely covered, taking care not to break the stems. If you wish, add a few snowdrops, too. If the carnations are not in full bloom you can carefully brush them open. Place the 'cake' on a pretty plate and water it from time to time. As a finishing touch, place a few beautiful Easter eggs and feathers on top.

Hey presto, an Easter cake!

Anemones, eucalyptus and a variety of tulips.

A simple bouquet

It is not always size that counts; small can be just as pretty.
And for a small bouquet, there is no need to buy roses with long
stems or flowers with the biggest blooms. Long-stemmed roses are
often more expensive and large heads can overpower a bouquet.
Instead, mix many different varieties or choose flowers whose
colours harmonise. A gift of flowers is always appropriate and says
so much more than words. Even children love flowers, but how
often do we give them a bouquet?

Many people buy cut flowers and are afraid of shortening them. True, the price you pay sometimes seems to depend on the length of the stem. But sometimes you have to adjust the flowers to suit the vase, like this one where the roses have been cut down to fit a small teapot. Your display will look extra special if one flower picks out the colour of the vase.

Mixed bouquet with tulips, ranunculus and Prunus amandel

Let there be greenery!

Nerine (a relative of the amaryllis), snowball bush and pink and white cornflowers.

Welcoming and scented, lily of the valley in a pretty little basket made of cardboard hangs on the door. The flowers stand in a jar filled with water.

Sweet 'grandmother' flowers

Mention peonies and everyone says 'Oh, I love peonies!' Are they so appealing because they are available for only a short period of time? Or is it just because they are incredibly beautiful? The peony is a summer favourite for many people, grand and lovely enough to be in a vase all by itself. Sweet peas are just as lovable; heavenly scented and wonderful in bouquets.

Sweet peas and smooth lamb's ears makes a velvety bouquet.

To the one I love...

The scent of sweet peas takes me back to my childhood. Because I was born in July my grandparents always gave me a bouquet of marigolds, sweet peas and cornflowers. The bouquet would be tied in haste with a small piece of string. You can easily make someone just as happy with sweet peas. Nothing else is needed.

41

Anemone (Anemone coronaria)

Wonderful is also brief. The anemone is not long-lived, but what does that matter? If you like something you should allow yourself to enjoy it while it lasts. There are different varieties of anemone and they are available all year round. Those found in flower shops are mainly blue, red or white. They are sensitive, so take care when carrying them home.

Care and conditioning
- Cut the stems diagonally with a sharp knife.
- Place the flowers in cold water.
- Change the water frequently.
- Avoid direct sunlight.

Lily of the valley (Convallaria majalis)

What could be lovelier than a bouquet of sweet-scented lily of the valley? Few other flowers bring back so many memories and feelings of nostalgia. Nowadays you can buy small bouquets of lily of the valley in the flower shop for graduation day. As a child I would make my own bouquets of lily of the valley and small violets for my teacher at school. Bear in mind though that lily of the valley is poisonous. Always wash your hands after handling and make sure small children do not drink the flower water.

Care and conditioning
- Cut the stems with a sharp knife.
- Place the flowers in cold water.
- Change the water frequently.
- Store the flowers in a cool place during the night to keep them fresh.

Sweet pea (Lathyrus odoratus)

These lovely creations look like colourful butterflies. Our lord must have been in the best of moods when he created the sweet pea. It is beautiful on its own but also pretty with small roses, lamb's ears or marguerites. Sweet peas come in many shades of red, purple, pink and white.

Care and conditioning
- Cut the stems diagonally with a sharp knife.
- Place the flowers in cold water.
- Store the flowers in a cool place during the night to keep them fresh.

Narcissus (Narcissus)

Narcissi symbolise spring, the time of hope. There are many different varieties, large and small, including daffodils, white narcissi, and French daffodil, and they can be bought from January to April. On occasion the flower shop may delight you with unusual varieties; the sight of old-fashioned narcissi is particularly uplifting.

Care and conditioning
- Cut the stems diagonally with a sharp knife.
- Before you arrange narcissi with other flowers place them in a separate vase of cold water to remove the sap.
- Like all bulb flowers, they benefit from being stored in a cool place during the night.

Peony (Paeonia)

The peony is an exquisite cut flower that comes in many shades, from wine-red to cerise, pale pink and white. Peonies are lovely in a mixed bouquet

narcissus, peony, ranunculus, rose, tulip

but being so grand, they work perfectly on their own. They can also be dried. Hang them individually and they keep their wonderful shape. Peonies can be found in flower shops from May until July, and they last for about one week.

Care and conditioning
- Remove all leaves that would otherwise end up below the water level.
- Cut the stems diagonally with a sharp knife.
- Place the flowers in cold water.
- Change the water periodically.
- Store the flowers in a cool place during the night to keep them fresh.

Ranunculus (Ranunculus asiaticus)
The ranunculus is becoming ever more popular. It is pretty on its own but goes well in a mixed bouquet. The colours range from subdued white to flamed red, orange and yellow. Select those flowers whose buds have just started to show colour. They are available all year round. Ranunculus, by the way, means small frog in Latin.

Care and conditioning
- Remove all leaves that would otherwise end up below the water level.
- Cut the stems diagonally with a sharp knife.
- Place the flowers in cold water.
- Change the water frequently.

Rose (Rosa)
You can never have too many roses and here we're not just talking about red roses. The rose family has so many different personalities: rich, slim, round, tight, dark and light blooms – each as lovely as the next. The scent of some roses can be heavenly: deep and intoxicating. Roses are for many people the flower of love and around St Valentine's Day enormous quantities are sold. It is the most sold cut flower in Holland. Roses are available all year and keep for 3–14 days. If any stems should snap, cut off the flower heads and place them in a bowl of water or scatter the petals over the table. You can also drop them in the bath and invite your loved one to share.

Care and conditioning
- Remove all leaves that would otherwise end up below the water level.
- Cut the stems diagonally with a sharp knife.
- Place the flowers in lukewarm water.
- Change the water regularly.
- If the flower heads droop, re-cut the stems, wrap them in paper and place in fresh lukewarm water.

Tulip (Tulipa)
The tulip is a bulbous plant and there are plenty of varieties to choose from: single, double, feathered or fringed, lily-shaped and scented. One variety, the Parrot tulip, owes its feathery aspect to a virus. During the seventeenth century the tulip was exclusively for the rich, and a much sought-after commodity. Tulips are sold from October to May but their main season is January–April. Buy flowers that have just started to show colour.

Care and conditioning
- Leave any plastic around the tulips for about an hour.
- Cut the stems with a sharp knife.
- Place the flowers in cold water but don't give them too much; the more water, the more they drink and grow in length (though the length is of course a matter of taste.)
- Store the flowers in a cool place during the night to keep them fresh.
- Change the water every day.

Life is a party

When you throw a party you want to make things pretty for your friends. Unfortunately you often run out of time and need to put most of your energy into the food. But you can still impress your guests by laying the table festively: a well-ironed tablecloth, fancy china and especially flowers. For a party outdoors, you could hang a chandelier in a tree and decorate it with flowers and leaves. Choose flowers that can stay out of water for a while, such as chrysanthemum and ivy, and you won't need to wish for rain!

Fragrant lilac, sweet pea and
snowball bush give a summer
feeling to the table.

Wind a tendril of ivy around your napkins to decorate your place settings. It only takes a few seconds.

The table is ready!

Blue aconite sets the tone for a happy and delightful meal in the garden. Put them in a tall vase to look their best, for once placed to one side so that you can see all your guests round the table. Colourful cushions and bunting in the trees bring a feeling of gaiety.

I am childishly fond of bunting and would love to have the garden full. A yellow dahlia pegged out to dry makes the bunting extra decorative.

Aquilegia is an old-fashioned flower that often used to adorn the front of farmhouses and cottage gardens. It is not so common in flower shops but you can ask your florist to order them in season (spring and summer). Aquilegia comes in many different colours and there are both single and double varieties.

Rural charm

Wedding thoughts

The decision to wed marks a big event. Many couples choose to marry in summer when nature is making her own grand show and the sun is hopefully shining from a clear blue sky... You can, if you wish, let the season and the style of the wedding dictate the choice of flowers. Trendy or romantic? Classic or modern? Flower shops often keep portfolios to provide inspiration. The bold bride makes her own wedding bouquet and flower arrangements, if time allows....

A classic wedding bouquet with white roses, white astilbe and gypsophila
set in the green and white leaves of hosta.

For place-setting bouquets and the groom's buttonhole you can use the same flowers as in the wedding bouquet. Hide the binding by tying a thin green leaf around the flowers. Small bouquets also make beautiful decorations on gifts.

The bridesmaid's tiara is adorned with gypsophila.
Simply make mini-bouquets of gypsophila and use
fine wire to weave them around the whole tiara; the
flowers will last until long after the party has ended.
The halo is made from the soft down of a swan and
something that only angels have....

55

A summer garland

Making garlands for a party is a piece of cake – all you need is some fine wire and a pair of pruning shears. Use long tendrils of ivy (or potted ivy) for the base and decorate with marguerites and cornflowers. Make a mini-bouquet from a marguerite and a cornflower then wind it around the ivy vine with some wire. Continue to attach new bouquets evenly spaced along the ivy. For a long garland, tie several vines together or you can cheat a little and simply lay them in a line so that it looks as though they are attached.

A suggestion: if you are making the garlands a little in advance, you can keep them fresh by spraying them with water and placing them in a plastic bag in the fridge.

You can use the same flowers as a theme for everything from the wedding bouquet and hair decorations to the table decorations. For a romantic wedding theme, freesia and sprigs of cherry blossom look very pretty.

It's easy to make your own coiffure if you choose the right flowers. Freesia and gypsophila will both stay fresh for a day. The beautiful lace ribbon hides the pins used to attach the flowers.

Coffee cup dreams

The petals of ranunculus look like fluffy vanilla custard in this delightful cup decoration – and how beautiful strewn around the saucer! Be careful not to break the flower when removing the outer petals.

Simple and sophisticated, this little bouquet consists of roses in three different shades. It is quite unusual to mix different coloured roses, though you may well ask why when you see how good this sorbet-coloured composition looks.

To someone you love

Just think how love gives you butterflies! You might often buy red roses for your loved one but occasionally you may want to surprise them with something different. A humble muffin becomes a very special one with the help of some tiny bud roses and a flowery muffin case. Tie a beautiful ribbon around the paper case, toss some petals over the muffin and sprinkle some icing sugar on top. Yummy!

A romantic heart becomes a lovely table decoration. Soak a florist's foam heart in water for about an hour. Shorten the stems of ten or more carnations and insert them closely together in the foam to cover the entire surface. Try to select flowers that are in full bloom so that they completely cover the foam. Cover the sides with a beautiful lace ribbon and secure with a pin. Place the heart on a plate – don't forget to water it after a day or two.

Say it with carnations

The gift of love

Wrap your gift as you would normally then scatter it with rose petals. Carefully wrap the present in cellophane ensuring the petals stay in place. Decorate with a rosebud and a beautiful ribbon. If you have any petals left over sprinkle them in the bath, on the pillow or in front of the door before your guests arrive.

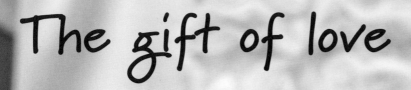

Roses and sweet peas are beautifully set off by the crochet-covered vase.

Cornflower (Centaurea cyanus)

The cornflower is the daisy's best friend. It comes in blue, pale pink, white and purple and is a true summer flower in Sweden. It reminds me of mid-summer garlands worn in the hair and of tall maypoles.

Care and conditioning

- Remove all leaves that would otherwise end up below the water level.
- Cut the stems with a sharp knife.
- Place the flowers in cold water.
- Change water frequently (it may start to smell).
- Store the flowers in a cool place during the night to keep them fresh.

Gypsophila (Gypsophila paniculata)

Gypsophila is perfect for those who want to make simple and playful arrangements. It suits every occasion, from small bouquets for children at a christening, to wedding tiaras and table decorations; the possibilities are endless. It is good for filling up bouquets and is also beautiful as a solitary flower – try just a few stems in a large glass vase. Gypsophila is long lasting and ideal for hair decorations since it looks almost the same fresh or dry. The most common variety you can buy today is called Million Star. On occasion you may find gypsophila coloured pink or blue. It's not for everyone, but in the right context it can be fun.

Care and conditioning

- Remove all leaves that would otherwise end up below the water level.
- Cut the stems with a sharp knife.
- Place the flowers in warm water.

Freesia (Freesia x hybrida)

The freesia is a much-underrated flower that deserves to be more popular as a modern cut flower. The wonderful scent can weaken anyone's knees, so use it to seduce yourself or someone else. The classic yellow freesia in particular has a magnificent fragrance. Freesias come in many different colours and they are really long lasting.

Care and conditioning

- Cut the stems with a sharp knife.
- Place the flowers in cold water.

Marguerite (Chrysanthemum grandiflorum)

Marguerites and daisies (Leucanthemum) belong to the chrysanthemum family.
Many people associate them with the height of summer, for what would it be without these little beauties? Marguerites are usually white and not quite as long lasting as other cut chrysanthemums, which can stay fresh for up to two weeks.

Care and conditioning

- Remove all leaves that would otherwise end up below the water level.
- Cut the stems diagonally with a sharp knife.
- Place the flowers in lukewarm water.
- Change water frequently as it easily becomes cloudy, and rinse the stems under water as they tend to be a little sappy.
- Store the flowers in a cool place during the night to keep them fresh.

ivy, carnation, snowball bush, aconite

Ivy (Hedera)

We normally find ivy as a potted plant, but keep an eye out for it sold in long tresses in some flower shops. It can last without water for some time, so you can have enormous fun with it; use it, for example, to dress the chandelier or twine as napkin rings, candle rings or garlands. Best of all, the unassuming ivy can really make a bouquet when you only have a few other flowers.

Care and conditioning
- For a bouquet or florist's foam decoration, cut the ivy stems with a sharp knife.
- Place the stems in lukewarm water.
- For table decorations or garlands, preferably made the day before, spray with water, enclose in a plastic bag and store in a cool place.

Carnation (Dianthus)

Dianthus means the joyous flower and I have to agree with that. The carnation has a reputation for being a funeral flower but it has so much more to give. It is versatile and long lasting, worth its price and above all incredibly beautiful. There are single- and multi-coloured carnations, large and small flowers, some with fragrance and some without. The small ones with several flowers on a single stem are called miniature carnations. Carnations are available all year and last for between one and three weeks.

Care and conditioning
- Remove all leaves that would otherwise end up below the water level.
- Cut the stems diagonally with a sharp knife.
- Place the flowers in lukewarm water.
- Change the water frequently and re-cut the stems every time.

Snowball bush (Viburnum opulus)

When sold as a cut flower the snowball bush is also commonly called viburnum. The small flowers are normally green when you buy them but turn white in full bloom. The Snowball bush is available all year but especially during spring. It is as beautiful in a mixed bouquet as in a single display.

Care and conditioning
- Remove all leaves that would otherwise end up below the water level.
- Cut the stems diagonally with a sharp knife.
- Place the flowers in lukewarm water.
- Store the flowers in a cool place during the night to keep them fresh.

Aconite (Aconitum)

If you are looking for flowers with authority you want, choose aconites. They are proud by themselves and work perfectly with other flowers. They make an excellent base for a large arrangement, teamed with luscious flowers such as peonies, eustomas (Lisianthus), lilies or carnations. Aconites are available in white, blue and two-toned blue and white. The flowers last for between five and seven days.

Care and conditioning
- Remove all leaves that would otherwise end up below the water level.
- Cut the stems diagonally with a sharp knife.
- Place the flowers in lukewarm water.

Autumn dreams

Carrying an armful of flowers wrapped in newspaper and dressed in a warm coat and scarf, I feel like an autumn version of someone straight out of the TV series Sex and the City. In autumn you can find swathes of large, elegant flowers in warm glowing colours and they are rarely expensive. So treat yourself to a big bunch of flowers from the flower shop or a market stall, fill your home with them, light some candles and curl up.

Dahlia, strelizia,
protea and eucalyptus
make a vividly coloured
bouquet.

The sunflower is the ultimate autumn flower. A single head in a vase is enough to make you feel enriched. With its powerful stalk, sun-yellow colour and velvety smooth seed-filled centre, it's not only the birds' favourite but also mine.

Don't be stingy with gladioli! The more you buy, the more magnificent the effect. Try mixing different but harmonious colours.

A fabulous bouquet for the hostess. Dahlia, snapdragon, pink cornflower and pink thistle (Cirsium) – a thorny beauty that comes in different colours.

The dahlia is the flower equivalent of Frida Kahlo: strong, vibrant and completely irresistible. And just like this artist, it comes from Mexico.

Sometimes unarranged
flowers can look surprisingly
beautiful. Roses, dahlias,
gerbera and rosehip are
soaking in a bucket.

So simple, so pretty

Less is more. Cut the stem off a gerbera and place on the napkin. Done!

Make your own cones from beautiful paper. Pop one or more gerberas or dahlias in glass tubes and place them in the cones. Fun to give away.

79

Chrysanthemums in a pumpkin

Ah, lovely, colourful and sweet-scented chrysanthemums! Come the autumn there are so many varieties to choose between, and they last for ages. A 3,000-year-old legend tells how the emperor of China ordered a few of his men to seek out a magic herb that would bring eternal youth. The men returned with some twigs of chrysanthemum. Eternal youth or not, chrysanthemum is now second only to the rose in terms of the numbers sold.

A pumpkin is transformed into a vase in this arrangement. Cut the top off the pumpkin and scoop out all the seeds and pulp. Place a suitable jar filled with water inside the hollowed-out pumpkin and fill with flowers.

When a bouquet is on its last legs there are often a few fresh flowers remaining. Simply shorten the stems with a sharp knife and place the flowers in different shot glasses. Suddenly, you have a whole new arrangement. Stand the glasses on the bedside table, in the bathroom or tuck them into unexpected places.

It looks great to mix
chrysanthemums
of different sizes
and colours in
a bouquet.

Calla lilies don't only come in white. In warm hues of purple, orange or yellow they make a less formal impression but are just as elegant. A bouquet for the modern autumn bride, perhaps?

Trick your dinner guests with these spidery Vesuvio chrysanthemums popped into small plastic bowls on the table. Also perfect for children's ghost parties.

Olé!

With a rustic tablecloth, mini flower 'cakes' and a few scattered carnation petals, the table gets a southern provincial touch. Soak a piece of florist's foam for about an hour and cut it into pieces to fit inside small bowls. Wrap the bowls with pretty paper or wallpaper and secure with raffia or string. Place the soaked foam in the bowls. Cut the stems of some roses and carnations to about 2–3 centimetres and press them gently into the foam. Don't forget to put a carnation behind your ear! Olé!

Fill a bowl with some pillow moss. String enough carnation heads on thin wire to form a ring that fits inside your bowl and place on the moss. Spray the moss with water. If you wish, add a decoration in the centre and a few long, thin candles.

A small bouquet with carnations and a needlepoint ribbon. Tie together about ten carnations making the knot high, almost under the flower heads. Cut the stems to leave just a short 'handle'.

Pure style, on a plate and in a vase

Fluffy carnations, dahlias and roses clustered on a plate.

Simple and professional: pretty pink
carnations in a pure white cylinder.
Cut the stems so that the flower heads
just hang over the rim of the vase.
Add flowers until the vase is packed full.

Dahlia, gerbera, gladiolus, chrysanthemum,

Dahlia (Dahlia x portensis)
Were the dahlia longer-lasting it would be the queen of cut flowers. Dahlias come in every colour and can be single or two coloured. Make the most of them in season, from August until the end of October.

Care and conditioning
- Remove all leaves that would otherwise end up below the water level.
- Cut the stems with a sharp knife.
- Place the flowers in cold water.
- Change the water frequently.
- Store the flowers in a cool place during the night to keep them fresh.

Gerbera (Gerbera x cantabrigiensis)
The gerbera is the perfect symbol of a flower. It looks like a child's first flower drawing: a stick, a dot and petals all around. Growers in Holland, where the gerbera is much in demand, are constantly trying to come up with new varieties; there are currently about 350 varieties in all colours except blue. Gerbera stems are soft and some florists support them with plastic or

thin wire; don't be tempted to remove this, although it doesn't matter if the flowers bend a little.

Care and conditioning
- Cut the stems diagonally with a sharp knife.
- Place the flowers in warm water, but not too much: only about 10 centimetres of the stem should be submerged, otherwise it will go soft. If the heads droop after a day or two, re-cut the stems and place in hot water.

Gladiolus (Gladiolus x hortulanus)
We can revel in gladioli with the arrival of autumn. They are not only beautiful but also well worth their price during this season. Gladioli come in a range of wonderful colours, not only white, pink and yellow but also pinky-orange, red and wine-red – exactly the tones of autumn. You can make a simple table arrangement by picking off the flowers and letting them float in small bowls of water.

Care and conditioning
- Remove all leaves that would otherwise end up below the water level.
- Cut the stems with a sharp knife.
- Place the flowers in cold water.
- Carefully nip off the top three buds. This encourages the other buds to bloom.
- Remove faded flowers.

Chrysanthemum (Dendranthema)
The chrysanthemum family is large and new varieties of different hues and shapes are constantly being introduced; today there are chrysanthemums in every colour but black. Chrysanthemums are really easy flowers to use. You can incorporate them in various arrangements, with other flowers or as a bouquet on their own. (You can also brew tea from the dried flowers and the drink is said to be effective against the 'flu). The glory days of the chrysanthemum are in autumn, but they are available all year round and the flowers can last for up to two weeks.

Care and conditioning
- Remove all leaves that would otherwise end up below the water level.
- Cut the stems diagonally with a sharp knife.
- Place the flowers in lukewarm water.
- Change the water frequently.

snapdragon, strelitzia, protea, sunflower

Snapdragon (Antirrhinum majus)

The snapdragon is a childhood favourite of mine. If you squeeze the sides of the little flowers their mouths open up. I thought it was really scary when I was little ... what could be hiding inside the mouth? These days I appreciate the snapdragon for its peculiar beauty and the fact that it combines so well with other flowers like the delphinium, peony, marguerite, lily, rose, or with green leaves such as lamb's ears and hostas. Snapdragons come in several colours.

Care and conditioning
• Remove all leaves that would otherwise end up below the water level.
• Cut the stems diagonally with a sharp knife.
• Place the flowers in lukewarm water.
• Change water frequently.

Strelitzia (Strelitzia reginae)

This sensational flower brings back memories of exotic places in the sun. It's one of the things tourists can buy in the Canary Islands airports. But it is a little tricky because it will not bloom by itself – in nature, this is done by birds; we have to ask the florist to help it along a little. Strelitzia are available all year and last for up to ten days.

Care and conditioning
• Cut the stalks diagonally with a pair of pruning shears.
• Place the flowers in lukewarm water.

Protea (Protea)

This is the national flower of South Africa. If you've ever visited that country and seen the protea in its natural environment you may already have an affinity for this unusual beauty. It looks like no other flower and many may think it difficult to combine with others. That scarcely matters since the protea is so majestically beautiful in its own right, but with some fresh creativity it can also look wonderful in a mixed arrangement.

Care and conditioning
• Remove all leaves that would otherwise end up below the water level.
• Cut the stalks diagonally with a pair of pruning shears.
• Place the flowers in warm water.
• Change the water frequently.

Sunflower (Helianthus annuus)

The classic autumn flower. The sunflower really does look like the sun, spreading warmth and joy, and a whole bunch makes you feel extremely happy! Sunflowers are so elegant you don't need many to make a stunning bouquet. They come in various gorgeous shades of yellow, red and brown, and last for about five days.

Care and conditioning
• Remove all leaves that would otherwise end up below the water level.
• Cut the stalks with a sharp knife.
• Place the flowers in lukewarm water.
• Remove even more leaves to allow extra nourishment for the flower.

Christmas is coming!

The time leading up to Christmas, before everything gets stressful, is lovely. I buy wreaths and decorate the entire house with flowers, not least hyacinths, for their scent is a must in December. Of course, it's lovely to have Christmas baskets and potted hyacinths but cut flowers can bring just as much Christmas spirit into the home. Why not release the traditional flowers like amaryllis and hyacinth from their pots and bulbs and use them in exciting different ways?
Try them with white orchids!

Christmas with a difference

Hyacinths are wonderful as cut flowers and smell divine, so why not do something different with them? Carefully remove the little bells from the stems and thread them onto a length of fine wire then shape it into a heart, a cross or whatever you fancy. Place the finished garland in a little water; it will stay fresh until you are ready to display it.

Still life with a hyacinth heart and candles. You could use a picture of your loved ones and make your own special 'altar'.

Hyacinth bells and beads threaded on wire make a sweetly scented napkin ring.

Anemones, hyacinths, white ranunculus and green fern fronds make a pretty hand-tied bouquet held with a beautiful ribbon.

Christmas sparkle

Revel in a little glamour at Christmas and let your flowers sparkle too. Buy a tube of glitter and sprinkle over your flowers – anemones in full bloom are perfect for this. Combine your sparkling flowers with waxed red pears rolled in sugar glitter. (Florists often stock waxed pears at Christmas.) The pears make an attractive display on the table along with a few hyacinth bells, red ranunculus and eucalyptus leaves.

Anemone pastries

Place small glass bowls inside muffin cases, and secure with string. Fill with water and pop a single anemone head into each bowl. A clematis vine taken from a potted plant provides the contrasting greenery.

Hold together the stalks of 4–5 amaryllis and wind a beautiful ribbon around them, working from the top to the bottom.

A Christmas arrangement with Asian elegance

Amaryllis, anemones and eucalyptus stylishly displayed in a Chinese pot. Cut the stalks to an appropriate length and pack them tightly together in the pot.

Winter beauty

An arrangement using red amaryllis, bilberry sprigs and white orchids. Fill a bowl with soaked florist's foam. Cut the stalks to an appropriate length and place the flowers one by one into the foam. To prevent the amaryllis stalk from curling, attach a rubber band at the base of the stalk and make a hole in the foam before you press it into place. For a less expensive display, just use fewer flowers and more foliage.

Brighter times

The minute Christmas is over I want spring to arrive! It is a new year with new plans and lots of new energy. Everything red is out; instead the mood is for all things light and airy. It's time to buy flowers in light colours: the lily, iris, calla and, yes, amaryllis too, but in white or pastel shades. Brighter times are ahead again. How lovely!

A single iris in a champagne glass.

Look deep into the beautiful eye of the anemone with its seductive fringes. A true Asian beauty.

The alstroemeria too is worth a closer look, with its soft round petals and delicate tracery. Here, for once, it gets all the attention.

A garland does not have to be worn on the head. In many countries beautiful garlands are made to be worn around the neck. We used eustomas (Lisianthus), broom and hazel catkins threaded together with soft white feathers.

A delicate silver birch wreath holds eustomas in small glass tubes. You can buy birch twigs, sprayed in different colours, in many flower shops. Gently bend the twigs into the shape you require and fasten with wire.
Use beautiful ribbons to tie the glass tubes to the wreath, fill them with water and place two or three flowers in each one. Decorate with paper flowers, birds or anything else that inspires you and then hang the wreath from the ceiling.

Fritillaries with birch twigs sprayed baby pink. The small water-filled glass tubes are attached with a checked ribbon.

A hydrangea head decorates this little wrapped box. Today you can buy hydrangea as a cut flower. Its shape and colour make the hydrangea seem slightly old fashioned, so it works perfectly for traditional occasions such as weddings and christenings.

115

Amaryllis are not
only for Christmas!
The white and pink
varieties are beautiful
spring flowers.

Place a single white carnation on a napkin and toss a few petals over the plate. Your guest can take the babushka doll home.

Calla lilies make gorgeous table decorations, the pink ones for the gentlemen and the white ones for the ladies. Tie a length of silk ribbon around each one and lay one on each place setting.

Calla lilies for six

Chinese porcelain filled with white ranunculus

A quirky 'Alice in Wonderland' arrangement with lilies, ranunculus and gypsophila brimming over the teapot.

Alstroemeria (Alstroemeria)

This flower has been around in flower shops for a long time but quite anonymously. It was once common on the tables of restaurants, probably because it's so long lasting. We'd like to push for the alstroemeria, since it now comes in exciting new colours and it looks so lovely in a mixed arrangement. Its origins are apparent from its common name, Peruvian lily, but today alstroemeria are being cultivated in Sweden and we want to support that. The flowers are available all year round and they last for up to two weeks. Alstroemeria took its name from Clas Alströmer, a pupil of Carl von Linné.

Care and conditioning
- Remove all leaves that would otherwise end up below the water level.
- Cut the stems diagonally with a sharp knife.
- Place the flowers in cold water.
- Change the water frequently.
- Nip off faded flowers to encourage fresh ones to bloom.

Amaryllis (Hippeastrum)

The amaryllis is a bulbous plant that has become increasingly popular as a cut flower. New varieties and colours are being introduced each year and there seems to be no end to the inventiveness of the breeders: there single and double amaryllis, large or small bells, striped and streaked ones and they come in red, purple, orange, pink and white. The amaryllis is such a grand flower in its own right it scarcely needs other flowers. Even so, a little foliage, like olive branches or eucalyptus, can look beautiful. When you buy amaryllis there is often a stick inside the stalk and a rubber band at the end. Leave these in place: the stick supports the stalk and the rubber band prevents it curling up. The season for amaryllis is September until the end of May but it is most common around Christmas. It lasts for up to two weeks.

Care and conditioning
- Cut the stalk with a sharp knife.
- Change the water frequently.
- The pollen can stain but you can remove it from your tablecloth or clothes by gently dabbing it with a piece of tape.

Eucalyptus (Eucalyptus)

The eucalyptus is a loyal friend, one who has been in the flower business for a long time. With its spicy fragrance and beautiful grey-green foliage it perfectly complements cut flowers. Eucalyptus grows as a bush or a tree. It stays fresh for about two weeks if you re-cut it and change water frequently.

Care and conditioning
- Remove all leaves that would otherwise end up below the water level.
- Cut the stalk with a sharp knife.
- Place the stalks in lukewarm water.

Hyacinth (Hyacinthus)

We are used to buying hyacinths as bulbs, but increasingly they are sold as cut flowers. Choose light pastel colours for a gorgeously scented spring bouquet. In the eighteenth-century Madame Pompadour, the mistress of Louis XV, created a new fashion for necklaces made out of hyacinth bells, her favourite flower.

Care and conditioning
- Cut the stems with a sharp knife.
- Rinse any sand from the stems.
- Place the flowers in cold water.
- Change the water frequently. Too much sap in the water will smell!
- Store the flowers in a cool place during the night to keep them fresh. If you intend to make a necklace from the bells, store it in a plastic bag in the fridge until you need it.

Iris (Iris x hollandica)

Surely it's time to banish the idea that a bouquet for a special occasion should consist of yellow roses and blue irises? Think of all those other lovely ideas for bouquets. Maybe it's worth giving the iris another try, minus the yellow roses? With its exotic shape and array of colours – yellow, cream, white, purple and blue – it looks almost like an orchid and is perfect displayed in its own right. Iris can be bought all year round.

Care and conditioning
- Cut the stems diagonally with a sharp knife.
- Place the flowers in cold water.

Calla lily (Zantedeschia)

For the older generation, the calla lily may be seen as a funeral flower. Luckily, younger people view it differently. Its simple, elegant form and colours make it a trendy choice for decorating the modern home. The demand is such that calla lilies are now available all year round in various colours: white, wine-red, orange and brown.

Care and conditioning
- Handle carefully as the flower is easily bruised.
- Cut the stems with a sharp knife.
- Place the flower in lukewarm water.
- Change the water frequently.

Lily (Lilium)

Like the calla, the lily was once much used in funeral arrangements, especially the Easter lily (Lilium longifolium). Nowadays these beautiful flowers, some of them scented, enjoy a much wider showing, and rightly so. If you buy lilies wrapped lilies in plastic they make a more luxurious gift if you remove the plastic and tie them with a beautiful ribbon. They are available all year. To avoid stains from the pollen you can nip off the anthers once the flower has opened.

Care and conditioning
- Remove all leaves that would otherwise end up below the water level.
- Cut the stems diagonally with a sharp knife.
- Place the flowers in lukewarm water.
- Change water frequently.

Lisianthus (Eustoma grandiflorum)

This is a popular cut flower that is much seen in flower shops. It comes in white, cream, pink and purple shades as well as a bold two-colour variety. Eustoma is a beautiful flower to use on its own. Many florists still sell it under the old name, lisianthus or prairie gentian, but its scientific name is eustoma. It keeps for up to a week.

Care and conditioning
- Remove all leaves that would otherwise end up below the water level.
- Cut the stems with a sharp knife.
- Place the flowers in cold water.
- Remove faded flowers to encourage the new buds to blossom.

Acknowledgements
Flower Council of Holland
R.o.o.m.
Alverbäcks
Tunvalla Garden centre
Årstiden
Ceannis
Lundholms Papper
Rice
Florahallen

And many flower cakes to Elisabeth Björkbom for the pretty design of this book.

Malin Hidesäter is a florist and has a well-known 'flower profile'. She has amongst many other things shared her ideas on the Swedish television DIY-series Äntligen hemma. Malin invites a playful relationship with flowers and plants. With her quirky imagination and creative zest she can make even the most traditional flower exciting.

Anna Skoog is a photographer with a passion for flowers and plants. She has taken pictures for several flower and gardening books, including Vårens lökväxter (Spring Bulbs), and photographed everything from snowdrops in her own garden to wild orchids in South Africa. Her other subjects include food and furnishings.